PARENTING HAN

*Helping you and your child
make sense of everyday
challenges together*

By Dr Sarah Mundy
Consultant Clinical Psychologist

Illustrations by Rachel Millson-Hill

Text and Illustrations copyright © 2020 Sarah Mundy

IBSN - 978-1-8380144-0-7

Printed and bound in China

www.parentingthroughstories.com

Dedications

Like having children, Parenting Through Stories has been a labour of love. I would like to dedicate this to my three wonderful boys. It is also dedicated to my mum, an unconditionally accepting and empathic parent, and my dad, whose playfulness and storytelling has brought me great joy.

Finally, this book, and the accompanying series of children's stories, Bartley's Books, would not have been possible without the experiences I have had working therapeutically with so many amazing children and parents over the years. Each family has enhanced my understanding of a child's need for nurture, connection, and unconditional love, as well as for a caregiver who can help them to make sense of their lives. I would like to thank them for this.

CONTENTS ──────────────

Introduction..7

Why a Parenting Handbook?...................................7-9

Aims of the Stories.. 9-10

How to Use the Books...11-13

The Importance of Storytelling............................14-16

Trying out Some Ideas in Your Parenting...................17

Looking After Yourself...18

What is it Like to be a Young Child?.....................19-20

Parenting and Brain Development.............................21

The Attachment Relationship....................................22

The PACE Model..23-31

Rupture and Repair..32

Emotional Development..33-34

Encouraging Positive Behaviour..35

Managing Tricky Behaviour..36-39

Managing Yourselves During Tantrums................................40-41

The Importance of Play (as well as Playfulness)......................42-43

Separation Anxiety...44-45

The Arrival of a New Sibling..46-48

Mastering New Skills and Establishing Routines....................49-50

Bedtime Routines...51-53

Healthy Eating..54-57

Toilet Training...58

Children with Additional Needs...59-60

Top Tips:

Separation Anxiety...62-64

Tricky Behaviour...65-68

The Arrival of a New Sibling............................69-71

Bedtime Routines...72-74

Healthy Eating..75-77

Toilet Training...78-80

For Parents...81-83

About the Author and Illustrator....................84-85

References..86-88

Reviews..89-90

Acknowledgements...91-92

Introduction

I am Dr Sarah Mundy, mother of three young boys and a practising Consultant Clinical Psychologist. I specialise in working with children and families, and through this have learnt a great deal about those things that help (and hinder) family life, as well as ways to promote positive child development.

After having my first child I read a number of parenting books and found they often offered conflicting advice, which was rarely supported or explained by relevant theory. What surprised me most was the lack of a story or a voice for the child within such books. It felt as though parents were told what to *do* to their child to make changes, rather than how to work *with* their child to make things easier. I felt that it would have been helpful to have some books to read with my children to enable them to make sense of common, but tricky, situations that they faced. I couldn't find any - hence the birth of Bartley's Books and the wider Parenting Through Stories approach.

Why a Parenting Handbook?

Over the last few years, there seems to have been a positive shift within parenting books from a focus on managing children's behaviour to understanding and supporting their inner world – their thoughts, feelings and sense of self.[1] This handbook provides a background to Bartley's Books, describing the approaches I have taken in writing the stories and considering the challenges that each story addresses. It also discusses children's emotional and behavioural development more generally and gives you some additional ideas to put into practice in your day-to-day parenting.

I know you have oodles of information about parenting at your fingertips. I did not want to bombard you with what you 'should' do as a parent, so have written this handbook in short sections with suggestions, rather than directions, for you to draw upon if you feel they would be beneficial to your family. You don't need to read this handbook cover to cover before sharing the stories with your child – the key to Parenting Through Stories, which is different from other parenting approaches out there, is the interactive element of Bartley's Books.

The shared reading experience gives you tools to help you and your child understand and manage everyday challenges, as well as to spend more enjoyable, connective and reflective moments together.

Use this handbook as it suits you – dip in, read it in short bursts, or flick to the parts you feel are most relevant to you. There are a number of references throughout which direct you to research reviews, relevant books and websites if you are interested in exploring a particular topic further. If time is limited (which it normally is with little ones around), do concentrate upon moments to interact with your child, rather than reading about theoretical approaches.

As well as suggestions on how best to read Bartley's Books with your child, this handbook contains some overarching ideas to enhance your parenting. I have focused on attachment theory (drawing primarily on Dan Hughes' PACE model[2]) and storytelling, and describe how these are important for children's development and their ability to manage their feelings, behaviour and relationships.

Information on what it feels like to be a young child (of around two to four years old) is included to help you consider your child's perspective and what support they may need. I hope this will give you additional insight into why some behaviour occurs which is frustrating (for both you and your child), and why it seems to take forever for them to learn what seems like a very straightforward task (like falling asleep).

At the end of the handbook, I have included some "Top Tips" in relation to each of the areas considered. These are also included in a condensed format at the end of each story in Bartley's Books, allowing you to consider a specific issue without having to cross-reference the handbook with the picture books.

I have used the word "parent" throughout this book. I am aware that children can have a number of important adults in their life, and that their primary carers may not be a mum and/or dad. Similarly, I refer to your child as "they" for ease of reading and to remove the need for gender specific terms.

We increasingly have different family make-ups, and I hope that you feel able to reflect upon your own family's unique circumstances when reading the stories with your child. As described later, the prompter questions in Bartley's Books can always be adapted according to your child's own experiences.

You may also want to share this handbook and Bartley's Books with others involved in looking after your child, such as childminders, teachers and grandparents. This will help different adults adopt a similar approach and have some tools at the ready to support your child through their early years.

Although Parenting Through Stories is aimed at younger children, with Bartley's Books written specifically with two to four-year-olds in mind, many of the ideas in this handbook are also relevant to older children. It is important to try not to worry if issues normally associated with the toddler years last longer, or start later, than you expect; children vary greatly in the ages at which they encounter and overcome different situations. I misguidedly thought I had escaped the 'terrible twos', only to find them all too present at three and a half (and still going strong!).

Aims of the Stories

In both my personal and professional experience, I have found that both pre-schoolers and older children need help in making sense of their world (as do we as adults), and stories are a powerful way to do this. I regularly use stories in my clinical work and see the positive impact they can have in helping children to understand and express themselves.

Bartley's Books feature Bartley the bear (and his parents) learning to cope with, and understand, his world. There's also a curious squirrel called Nudge around to help (he can be found by lifting the flaps). Throughout the stories, prompter questions asked by Nudge help your child to understand both Bartley's and their own experiences. They encourage interaction and help you to understand your child's perspective of the world. Think of the flaps as windows into your child's internal world that help them learn to reflect.

The stories consider a range of normal developmental experiences which parents (and their children) often find difficult to manage.

These include:

- **Separation Anxiety** – *Please Stay Here - I Want You Near*
- **Tricky Behaviour** – *Stop That Now - I Don't Know How*
- **The Arrival of a New Sibling** – *Hey, Little Mister - Meet Your Sister!*
- **Healthy Eating** – *Please Eat Up – No, It's Yuck!*
- **Toilet Training** – *You'll be Happy - Without Your Nappy*
- **Bedtime Routines** – *Time for Bed - Rest Your Head*

They are designed to support parents to help their child manage these situations, through learning to understand their feelings and behaviour, find new ways to cope with them, and better understand expectations and routines.

Bartley's Books aim to:

- Support young children's emotional and behavioural development and ability to think about their own and others' feelings.
- Help your child learn that they are not alone in finding some feelings and situations hard to manage.
- Give young children a space in which to think about their experiences and to help them create a clear story about their feelings and expectations in the everyday situations they encounter.
- Help you, as parents, to understand how your child may view the world.
- Facilitate communication between you and your child.
- Give you more confidence in tackling difficult issues and talking to your child about them.
- Model the PACE approach (outlined on pages 23-31).
- Provide opportunities for connecting with your little ones and having fun together.

When children feel understood and know what to expect in certain situations their behaviour becomes easier to manage (they may even start to manage it themselves!). This makes them more enjoyable to care for and helps bring you closer together.

How to Use the Books

> *"When I say to a parent, 'read to a child', I don't want it to sound like medicine. I want it to sound like chocolate."*
> (Mem Fox – Children's Author)

Reading the Stories with Your Child

Huge changes take place during the early years and children vary greatly in their language development (both understanding and spoken), as well as in the ages at which they face and overcome different situations. It is up to you whether you want to read the stories with your child when the issues are currently a part of their lives, or whether you want to prepare them for future challenges by reading all the stories, even if you have not yet encountered the situation. Young children love repetition, so rediscovering a book at a later stage is always valuable.

Whilst designed to support children to think about their own experiences the stories do not focus exclusively on these, but on Bartley's too. This gives children the choice of thinking about themselves and/or about others. Whether they include themselves or not when considering the prompter questions, the interactive element of the stories should be helpful to children in making sense of feelings and behaviour. My eldest actively avoids questions about feelings, so, whilst I may talk about them I do not always expect a response in relation to his own experiences; he generally prefers to talk about others (which, in itself, helps him understand himself better).

I want to stress here (and throughout) that you know your child best – be creative and flexible with the stories. They have been developed to promote discussion rather than to follow a rigid script. If you think your child would like different questions in relation to their own experiences then feel free to adapt the prompter questions.

If you want to leave out the questions completely then do so, or you can answer them yourself or add more…it's up to you. Your child may guide you in this by lifting the flap to find out what Nudge has to say.

Try to go at your child's pace – they may want to engage in thinking about the questions or may just want to hear a story. For younger children it may be helpful to read the full story first without showing them the flaps (if little hands allow!), helping them to get a sense of Bartley's experiences before adding Nudge's voice.

Although the books focus on tricky situations, try to keep the atmosphere light-hearted and playful – children learn best when they feel at ease and through stories that are engaging and fun. It is helpful if you convey the emotional content of the story non-verbally as well as verbally – this often comes naturally but it can be helpful to be aware of your non-verbal and verbal communication and how it can affect your child's experience and enjoyment.

Whether the stories involve a two-way verbal conversation is likely to depend on the age of your child and their desire to engage in talking about their experiences. Whether your little one adds to the conversation or not, try to look at their non-verbal feedback (for example, are they listening to you? are they distracted?), to consider whether what you are saying is making sense to them. Although two-year-olds may not say much (that seems relevant at least!), they often understand more than we think. They are likely to have ideas even though they might have problems expressing them. Stories like these help them develop the important skill of talking about tricky situations and expressing their ideas.

When my friend read *Please Stay Here – I Want You Near* to her toddler for the first time, her little girl clearly enjoyed the story, but did not seem to actively engage with the reflective questions. However, that night she went home and started re-telling her own version to a doll, following which she seemed to spend a couple of days digesting the story. She is now talking much more freely about her own experiences of separation anxiety and telling her mum when she misses her (something she hadn't done before).

Through seeing how your child responds to these books you should find it easier to learn about their inner world and to tune into their feelings and understanding of situations. You can then work through these together, developing a shared understanding and exploring with them how they view the world. You can also show them that you care how they feel, that you understand their worries, that you want to help them, and that you are able to do this.

I hope your children enjoy the characters and, with your help, will be able to relate the stories to their own experiences.

Bartley   Nudge

The Importance of Storytelling

"After nourishment, shelter and companionship, stories are the thing we need most in the world."
(Philip Pullman – Author)

Think about your favourite story: how does it make you feel? what purposes does it serve?

Storytelling is a very powerful and important process for adults and children alike and can help children to:

• Understand their world and make sense of confusing situations.

• Develop a more positive sense of self (understanding of who they are).

• Understand their own and other people's feelings and behaviours.

• Feel more connected to others.

• Learn to communicate and problem solve.

There is a great deal of evidence that there are positive benefits of reading to, and making up stories with, children.[3,4,5] This includes the development of imagination, creative thinking, more cooperative behaviour, personal wellbeing, problem solving, self-confidence, social understanding and building an emotional vocabulary and understanding.

The world is a big place to young children who are still learning about rules and behaviour across a range of settings. Through stories we can help children understand what is expected of them. Talking with them about new experiences can make children feel more settled and teach them that their world can be predictable. We have little control over our lives when we are young. Telling stories together allows both you and your child to feel prepared for what lies ahead. You will learn about each other and be part of creating a new narrative.

We all make sense of our life through developing stories about it, and it has been found that people with more coherent narratives (organised stories) about their experiences have had more secure attachment relationships (which, as described later, are key to child development) and better emotional health.

Young children enjoy simple stories, rhymes, songs and a lot of repetition (even when we don't want to go over the same story again, and again, and again!). As with other things in life, young children need adults to help them make up stories and to learn how to tell them. There is often a particular narrative structure within stories, which is also seen in children's play before they are able to express this in words. This structure involves stories starting with a difficulty which is then resolved, and can be really helpful for children's longer-term problem-solving skills.

Telling your child stories will help them add words to play, provide them with a chance to relate other's experiences to their own lives, and help them realise that they are not alone in finding some things challenging. Stories which include explicit descriptions of feelings can help children make sense of, and accept, their own feelings, learn that emotions do not have to be overwhelming, and understand how others may feel.

When I make up stories with my children I am always amazed by what they bring to these, amused by their ideas and creativity and surprised by how much I didn't know about them. They provide me with insights into how they experience life, what they enjoy (mainly trains, tractors and helicopters) and what they need support with. We just have to remember to give our children the time and an opportunity to get involved.

Including children in creating stories with you enhances *intersubjectivity*: "The sharing of subjective states by two or more individuals."[6] This shared emotion, attention and intention helps children to understand that they can have an influence on others, as well as their own experiences. Moments of intersubjectivity deepen your emotional connection and are important for children's development.

It took me a long time to really understand what intersubjectivity meant. For me, the best way to understand it is moving away from experiencing the world separately, as *me* and *you*, to having shared experiences and goals together as *we*.

Telling stories together is a way to communicate and connect with each other - to find that *we* time. Story time can also be part of developing your special bond - children thrive on reading with their parents. I really hope that Bartley's Books help you feel more confident to connect with your child through stories, and help you to make sense of their experiences together.

Trying out Some Ideas in Your Parenting

In addition to reading the stories with your child, try to put some of the ideas into practice outside the storytelling process.

This suggestion comes with an admission: despite my knowledge of the theory behind the PACE approach to parenting (more about this later), and seeing it work in my clinical practice, I know it can be very hard to always keep up a calm and containing, open and engaged, stance when parenting young children.

I can think of a number of times that I have not been in tune with my children's needs, and have struggled to help them make sense of what was happening when they were having a meltdown. This was not because I didn't want to, but because I felt too tired, busy, frustrated or bored with the often repetitive nature of parenting to do this.

Do try not to put pressure on yourself to do this 'perfectly' - this is impossible. Just try to think about some of these ideas in your day-to-day interactions with your child and see if any of the parenting suggestions outlined in this handbook are helpful. If you do 'get it wrong' (which is inevitable at times, however hard we try), you can always apologise to your child for not having understood what was going on. That way your child gets to see that mistakes happen, that they are not the end of the world, and that saying sorry can make things feel better.

Making some mistakes and then reconnecting with your child is actually important for their development. More about this in the "Rupture and Repair" section later in this handbook.

Looking After Yourself

> *"The one thing children wear out faster than shoes is parents."*
> (John J Plomp - Author)

I can't understate how important it is to remember to look after *yourself*. We all know that it is hard to look after others if we are not looking after ourselves (but again, sometimes this is difficult to put into practice). Although having children can bring great joy, parenting can also feel relentless, thankless and exhausting, and children quickly pick up on stress. It seems to me as though nowadays, as parents, we have less support around us, with more demands placed upon us, making the job even more difficult.

Make sure you eat and sleep properly, exercise, make time for yourself, talk to others and ask for help if you need it. Keeping a sense of humour during hard times is also really important – this coping strategy has been related to positive outcomes.

Try not to use the word *should* too regularly (it puts a lot of pressure on you) - change it to *could*. For example, when I reflect upon the (many) moments I have got things wrong in my parenting, I feel much better about myself and am more able to do it differently the next time if I tell myself I *could* have done something else rather than *should* have. Sounds simple but it is a really good way to lessen the telling off we can all give ourselves as parents.

Always remember that you are trying to do your best, and be kind to yourself. This may all sound obvious, and you may know, in theory, that it is important, but do take a minute just to think about your own self-care. If you are worried about being too focused upon yourself, remember it is not just about you, but what you are modelling to your children.

We all have particular buttons, based upon our own experiences of being parented, which can be pushed by our children's behaviour. If you notice a specific behaviour is triggering a strong reaction for you it is worth reflecting upon what this may relate to. It may be more of your own 'stuff' than that of your child's. If you feel that this is becoming a problem, and you are finding it hard to step out of your own feelings and into your child's shoes, it may be worth finding someone to talk to about this, be it a friend or a professional.

What is it Like to be a Young Child?

Can you remember what it was like to be
two, three, or maybe four years old?

Perhaps you have a few memories: but
can you remember how it actually felt?
I certainly can't!

So, how can we understand
a young child's experience?

A Young Child's World

Try to put yourself in your child's shoes as much as possible. Knowing them well and understanding what is driving their behaviour allows us to discover better ways to support their development and can enhance your relationship with them.

Take a step back and watch your little one for just five minutes – see if you can work out what they are thinking and feeling. You may be surprised what you learn about them.

Parenting and Brain Development

Within the first few years of life, the brain develops dramatically. In fact, the first five years are considered to be a critical period in brain development. Babies are born relying upon the lower part of their brain, which houses their survival system. This means that they don't have the tools to make sense of their environment and can only show basic responses like crying to express discomfort and thereby get their needs met. Children then start to develop the higher parts of their brain, which are responsible for making sense of their world, and developing some control over how they manage it. This can take some time!

What I find fascinating is how key a parent's response is in shaping children's brain development: with consistent and responsive parenting, children develop more healthy connections to the higher, thinking and reasoning parts of their brain. Using these parts of the brain allows children to start to understand and manage their feelings and behaviour.

The key message from neuroscience is that the brain does not develop in isolation, but through relationships. Tina Payne-Bryson and Dan Siegel have written a very accessible and practical book (*The Whole-Brain Child* [7]) for parents in relation to this, which I highly recommend. If you wish to delve deeper into this area then have a look at Dan Hughes' and John Baylin's *Brain Based Parenting*.[8]

The Attachment Relationship

Humans are very vulnerable when they are born and need a huge amount of investment from their parents (as you well know!). The emotional bond between a child and their parent is based on their need for safety, security and protection and is called an *attachment relationship.*[9] There is a lot written about the importance of the attachment relationship and it is seen as the building blocks of a child's development, helping them to grow socially, emotionally, behaviourally and intellectually.

Children who experience their parents as predictable, nurturing and available are more likely to develop what is known as a *secure attachment relationship*. Secure attachment relationships have been shown to promote brain development, help children cope with feelings, relate to others, learn how to calm themselves, and feel safe enough to explore and learn about social and physical environments. A big part of building a secure attachment is being *in tune* with your child i.e. noticing how they are feeling and behaving, and helping them to make sense of this (known in the trade as *attunement*).

Without responsive parenting throughout the early years, children often get stuck with difficult feelings, not knowing how to manage these and expressing them through unhelpful and unhealthy behaviour. They can start to develop what is called an *insecure attachment relationship* with their parents, and learn to either suppress their feelings and not ask their parents for help (known as *avoidant* attachment strategies) or overly express their needs, becoming clingy and lacking independence (known as *ambivalent* attachment strategies).

It is important to remember that what seems like unhelpful and unhealthy behaviour in toddlerhood is a normal part of a child's development, exploring the world and learning what is and what is not OK – this is not, in and of itself, a sign of an insecure attachment relationship (so don't worry!).

The
PACE
MODEL

The PACE Model

I'm very interested in attachment theory and have seen the benefits of using ideas from this both in my clinical work and in my parenting. I particularly value the PACE model, a parenting approach developed by Clinical Psychologist Dr Dan Hughes, and have tried to embed the PACE ethos into Bartley's Books. When reading the stories with your child see if you can work out how Bartley's parents and Nudge the squirrel are showing PACE within them.

PACE stands for:

• *Playfulness* • *Acceptance* • *Curiosity* • *Empathy*

Consistently having these qualities in your parenting is thought to facilitate the development of a secure attachment relationship, making you feel more connected with your child and making parenting less stressful and more rewarding. It helps your child to feel understood and allows you to work through difficult situations together. Not only do these qualities of parenting improve your relationship but they also support your child's emotional and behavioural development.

It is important to note that PACE is an interpersonal stance rather than a technique designed to manage just the tricky times. It is a useful attitude to have when parenting, but also more generally in life – trying to be "PACEy" with yourself, your children, partner, friends and colleagues can make things feel more manageable and enjoyable for everyone.

I will outline the four elements of the PACE approach in a bit more detail.

Playfulness

> *"Mix a little foolishness with your prudence: it's good to be silly at the right moment."* (Horace - Roman Poet)

Playfulness is about trying to keep communication positive, light and playful and having fun with your child. When parents are playful, children are more likely to feel that they are enjoyable to be around, which feeds into a positive sense of who they are. Being playful makes conflicts easier to manage (both for us and for our children) and it can be a good way of defusing difficult situations.

With Mum and Doug on board, Bartley steered around the bends. They **Zoomed** past a planet and overtook some friends.

As you can see in the illustration from *Please Stay Here - I Want You Near*, Bartley's mum is showing playfulness through joining in with Bartley's imaginative world, despite him being worried about going to school, providing a moment of connection and fun amongst more tricky feelings.

Acceptance

Acceptance is shown through letting your child know that you accept who they are, warts and all. Parents often tell me they are concerned that accepting certain behaviour does not deal adequately with it and gives the message to their children that they are allowed to act in this way. Acceptance is not about condoning tricky behaviour but about letting your little one know that you understand there are things (such as their thoughts, wishes and feelings), driving this, and that you accept this (and therefore them).

There can still be consequences, although these need to be age-appropriate and successful. Often the best are natural consequences where you let your child learn from their own actions rather than imposing an unrelated sanction. For example, if a child refuses to wear their coat out, despite you insisting that they should because it's cold, a natural consequence would be for them to go out without a coat on, and feel the cold - if you do this always bring a coat for them with you!

Using punitive sanctions, which don't help children make sense of their behaviour, can be really upsetting, rarely helps and often makes children feel misunderstood and disconnected from you. If you are going to make meaningful changes, accepting that your child's behaviour is communicating something (and is not just designed to annoy you), and trying to work out what this is, normally helps more than reactive, unconnected sanctions. I believe that we can sometimes have overly high expectations of young children.

I think this quote from the songwriter Jim Morrison beautifully sums up acceptance:

"A friend is someone who gives you total freedom to be yourself - and especially to feel, or not feel. Whatever you happen to be feeling at any moment is fine with them. That's what real love amounts to - letting a person be what he really is."

Here is an example of Bartley's mum showing acceptance in *Please Stay Here – I Want You Near*. She is still being clear that she has to leave, but is accepting and acknowledging that this is not easy for him.

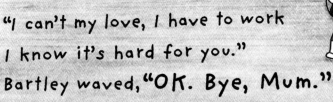

"I can't my love, I have to work
I know it's hard for you."
Bartley waved, "OK. Bye, Mum."
He didn't know what to do.

Curiosity

"Worlds can be found by a child and an adult bending down and looking together under the grass stems or at the skittering crabs in a tidal pool."
(Mary Catherine Bateson - Author)

Curiosity is about trying to understand what is going on for your child, letting them know you are interested in their internal world and working together to make sense of it. Once you accept that their behaviour is likely to be communicating feelings, showing curiosity helps both you and your child understand what the behaviour is likely to be about.

Helping children understand where their behaviour comes from and showing them alternative ways of managing it is likely to be more helpful in the longer term than putting in short-term behavioural consequences. Building an understanding of what is driving your child's behaviour will also help you feel less frustrated and more connected with them.

A lack of curiosity can lead to unhelpful interactions and negative feelings. As Kirsten Siggens (author) says: "When we aren't curious in conversations we judge, tell, blame and even shame, often without even knowing it, which leads to conflict."[10]

Remaining curious can be so helpful for children to learn that it is important to reflect on what is going on for them and to develop a non-shaming narrative about things they find hard. There is more about shame in the "Rupture and Repair" section of this handbook.

Nudge shows curiosity under the flaps in Bartleys Books. As shown below (taken from *Please Stay Here – I Want You Near*) Nudge is helping the reader make sense of both Bartley's and their own emotional experiences.

He looks really worried about going in - maybe he doesn't want to leave his Mum?

Do you sometimes feel like that?

Empathy

"It is an absolute human certainty that no one can know his own beauty or perceive a sense of his own worth until it has been reflected back to him in the mirror of another loving, caring human being." (John Joseph Powell - Author)

Empathy is a way of showing that you care about your child's world and that, when things are difficult, you are able to cope with their feelings, share them, and help them with these. As well as feeling cared for and understood, children who experience empathy from others develop this ability more quickly themselves - an important life skill.

As shown in the picture, Bartley's mum notices his anxiety, and shows him empathy, sharing it with him and giving him a cuddle (rather than dismissing it or trying to fix it).

Mum knew that he was worried and gave him a big bear hug.

Using PACE in your Parenting

Whilst the PACE approach sounds like a simple idea, it is sometimes easier said than done, particularly when we are having an 'off day'. I can think of a number of times when my lack of acceptance has hindered my own (and my children's) understanding and management of a difficult situation.

For example, I became quite cross with my middle child when we were away, expecting him to behave as well as the other children there. However, the other children had all slept in the afternoon whilst I was expecting my son to stay awake for longer than usual and to behave well while exhausted. These expectations were partly because I did not want him to look like a 'naughty' child to the other parents (he really was showing me up!) and because I wanted to socialise and not spend my time putting my son to bed. I, unhelpfully, blamed him for this.

It would have been more helpful if I had thought about why he was being difficult and acted accordingly, lowering my unrealistic expectations of him and accepting that it was unfair to expect him to be out and behave well when he was shattered (something which I struggle with myself when overly tired or stressed). This reminded me that all children are different, and that we need to think about, and accept, what they can manage and when they can manage it, rather than expect too much of them and then blame them for the consequences of not doing what we wanted.

It also highlighted to me that our own needs can get in the way of getting things right, and that, even with the best intentions, we do not always show acceptance. Looking after ourselves, repairing the relationship when we get it wrong, and thinking about our own strengths and vulnerabilities as parents can be useful at times like this.

It can be helpful to think about when you are least likely to use PACE in your parenting and which parts of the model you find the most difficult to put into practice – often this relates to our own experiences of being parented.

For example, I am much more accepting and playful than I am curious (which I can relate to my experiences of being parented); I therefore now try hard to stop and listen rather than switch to my default setting of thinking I know what is going on for my children. I am often surprised by how much more I learn about my boys when I do this and how, as a result, I feel more connected to them (and they to me).

If you are interested in reading more about the PACE approach see Kim Golding's book *Everyday Parenting with Security and Love: Using PACE to Provide Foundations for Attachment.*[11] As this model has been developed for children who have experienced early adversity, some of the information in Kim's book may not relate directly to your own child's experiences. However, I strongly believe that following this approach is helpful to all children, and that, at times, we can all benefit from a gentle reminder of which parenting qualities enhance ours and our children's lives. Indeed, when I have attended training with Dan Hughes he always reinforces the benefits of a PACE approach for all children and families, and the more I manage to put the PACE attitude into practice in my own parenting, the better our family seems to function, and the happier we all seem to be.

Rupture and Repair

"Love is a constant process of tuning in, connecting, missing and misreading cues, disconnecting, repairing and finding deeper connection. It is a dance of meeting and parting and finding each other again. Minute to minute and day to day." (Dr Sue Johnston - Psychologist)

There are many ruptures in our relationships with our children, particularly in toddlerhood, when we have to put in boundaries to keep them safe and help them learn about behaviour. When you repair your relationship with your child after a rupture this is believed to be helpful, in that they will feel 'mild' shame about what they have done wrong, but will learn that they are still loved regardless of this.

This leads to building more secure and trusting relationships and is part of developing the feeling of guilt - a positive emotion which allows a child to develop pro-social behaviour whilst not feeling bad about who they are. Without such repairs there is the risk that shame, a feeling that you (rather than the unhelpful behaviour you have shown) are bad, will become more prominent.

As we all know, shame is an incredibly uncomfortable feeling from which we just want to escape, making it hard to learn when we are feeling it. The more shame a child feels, the more they will protect themselves from it through unhelpful behaviours such as lying, minimising, blaming others and getting angry (known as the *shield of shame*).

So, the key is to set boundaries, and to follow through with them even if they lead to a rupture, but always try to mend your relationship afterwards so your child does not associate these ruptures with them being a bad person. **This is one of the most important tasks of toddlerhood: to be able to learn what is and what is not OK whilst, at the same time, feeling positive about yourself**. Your response, as parents, helps this process along. You will make mistakes (which are helpful in moderation) and have moments of disconnection with your child (particularly during toddlerhood), but repairing your relationship after these is very important.

Emotional Development

Young children struggle to hold onto their strong feelings without showing them (normally through behaviour). They can be quite overwhelmed by their emotions, feeling confused and out of control (picture the last tantrum you observed). Triggers to these feelings and related outbursts can also be quite confusing for parents; I certainly found it difficult to understand why my son felt that one sock being two centimetres lower than the other was a catastrophe! Young children need help to make sense of what they are feeling and to notice how this is connected to sensations within their bodies. They don't automatically have the words to know and explain what is going on and need adults to provide these for them.

As parents we can forget that children need help managing their emotional worlds, as well as their behavioural and physical ones. It is important that they are supported in identifying their feelings and that they have help in making sense of why they are getting frustrated, angry, sad and so on. I always encourage parents to name the feelings that their child may be struggling with but which are often left unsaid. Not naming difficult feelings often has a valid reason: because no one wants to stir them up or 'open a can of worms'. However, this can result in children feeling confused, misunderstood or bad for having such feelings.

It's really important not to dismiss what your child is feeling, but to take it seriously. I often hear parents, with the best intentions, telling their children "don't be silly" or not to worry. Whilst this is an attempt to make everything bright and bubbly, it does minimise the importance of their emotions and might make your child feel that you don't understand when they are finding things hard.

Bartley's Books model some ways in which you can label your child's feelings in a helpful way. Reading these stories with your child provides a space to talk with them about how they may have been feeling at particular times. This can be most helpful at a calmer time in the day, when they are feeling comfortable and relaxed; it is much easier to learn if we are not feeling angry or unsettled.

Sharing stories about tricky experiences and associated emotions with your child will help you develop a common language to discuss difficult feelings and understand each other's perceptions of events. For example, when you go to work your child may feel that this is because you don't want to be with them. Explaining this by saying you go to work because you enjoy it and you need to pay for food and toys, but that you still love being with them (even if going to work feels like a well-earned break!), can provide a different understanding about you being away and let them know that you still love them and want to spend time together. Something as simple as this might reduce the level of separation anxiety that they feel.

It is not just their own feelings that young children find hard to understand and articulate; they also struggle to understand what others feel. Because of this they are unlikely to consider your feelings when going about their daily lives. Young children start to really understand that other people have minds of their own (known as developing a *theory of mind*) at around the age of three or four, although even infants show some behaviours which represent the beginnings of this skill (see Astington & Edward, 2010, for further information on the development of theory of mind in early childhood).[12]

Not surprisingly, the timeframe for the development of theory of mind is not set, and varies according to children's experiences. For example, it has been found that children show earlier awareness of mental states if their mothers talk about thoughts, feelings and desires and provide reasons when correcting behaviour.[13] Children who experience parenting that is responsive and containing (when children feel safe and understood), where feelings are mirrored (when an adult is in tune with their children's emotions and reflects these back to them) and discussed, are likely to develop this skill more quickly than others.

Try to remember that young children are not very good at understanding that others have feelings too and that, even if they do understand this, they are not always motivated, or able, to act upon this knowledge.

Encouraging Positive Behaviour

Waiting for something is difficult for young children. They are often quite impulsive and can try to get what they want (such as a toy) through physical means (like snatching) as opposed to asking. Children's behaviour can get much worse at certain times; for example, they may find it particularly hard to manage their behaviour when they are tired and hungry. One of our (many) roles as parents is to help children learn to cope without becoming overwhelmed. This includes teaching them what is, and what is not, appropriate, giving them reasons for this, and understanding that they cannot always put this advice into practice.

Although we can get pulled into negative interactions quite quickly, it is important that children do not hear "don't" and "no" too often. (Easier said than done; I sometimes feel that I tell my middle child to stop doing something practically every minute of the day). Frequently telling a child not to do something can make them feel that the world is a negative place and that nothing, including exploring (which is key to learning), is allowed. In addition to teaching children what they should not do, we also need to teach them what they *can* do; we need to create opportunities for success and reward our children by noticing their achievements.

To help a child feel more in control of their behaviour, and not to feel like they are a bad person when they are being 'naughty', it is important that problems are seen as being separate from them. This is known as *externalising*. This lets them know that it is not them but what they are doing that you disapprove of. Externalising makes it more likely that your child develops a more positive self-image, whilst also addressing behaviour that is not acceptable (think back to the development of shame and guilt, outlined earlier in the "Rupture and Repair" section of this handbook). I certainly find it easier to reflect upon my behaviour when it doesn't feed into feeling that there must be something wrong with me as a person/parent. Externalising makes it easier to work on changes together and reduces the likelihood that children will feel at fault for things over which they have little control (yet).

Managing Tricky Behaviour

> *"Tantrums are not bad behaviour. Tantrums are an expression of emotion that became too much for the child to bear. No punishment is required. What your child needs is compassion and safe, loving arms to unload in."*
> (Rebecca Eanes - Author)

Tantrums are normally about what children think they need then and there. You may be surprised to learn that tantrums can actually be helpful in learning about managing feelings – a child who does not express big feelings may find it more difficult to tolerate frustrations in later life. Even though tantrums can be useful, and are part of normal development, young children do need help in managing them. Children can find the changes in their mood so sudden, confusing and overwhelming that they may find it hard to calm down. This can be frightening for children (as well as for parents).

It can be confusing how children can manage well in some situations, whilst in other, similar, situations they can have a huge meltdown. Behaviour and capacity for self-control can fluctuate markedly and it can take some time to work out what this is about. Young children have little common sense and have difficulty generalising, meaning that they may have learnt something in one situation, which, to us, is obviously applicable in a different situation, but not to them!

Tricky behaviour invariably communicates something, such as hunger, tiredness, boredom, physical illness, frustration, disappointment, lack of structure or understanding or difficulties at home. Your job is to work out what the trigger is this time and try to address the underlying concern (rather than just focus upon the difficult behaviour that arises from it).

Margot Sutherland, Child Psychotherapist, talks about different types of tantrums which may need different responses.[14] She describes distress tantrums, where a child is overwhelmed by their feelings and cannot talk or listen well.

In such situations a parent's job is to soothe through simple and calm actions and, if possible, distract and divert. During distress tantrums your child needs you close to them.

Little Nero tantrums refer to when your child tries to control their world but is not feeling genuine distress. Children use the tantrum to get what they want and are able to talk during it. The best way to respond to this is by not rewarding the behaviour (do not give them too much of an audience or give into their demand) and being firm and clear. Do reward your child with attention after the tantrum is over and remember that Little Nero tantrums can turn into distress tantrums, making our tuning in even more important in order to determine the best response.

One of the key aspects to Parenting Through Stories is the importance of having a connected relationship with your child. This could not be more true than during tricky times. Children are much more likely to react positively to your responses to their behaviour if they trust you and feel understood. Tina Payne-Bryson and Dan Siegal advocate a "connect then redirect" approach and Kim Golding talks about "connection before correction" in managing tricky behaviours.[11] For further information on how to "connect and redirect", have a look at *No Drama Discipline* (Payne-Bryson and Siegal), which provides easy to understand and realistic ways to do this.[15]

I would add "repair and reflect" (when the moment is right) to this approach. It might be helpful to reflect both on your own and together with your child. This will help you both learn from what happened and think about what you could do next time to reduce the chances of another meltdown.

When thinking about how to manage tricky behaviour, particularly distress tantrums, try to take the following approach:

Tricky Behaviour

Step Back

- Check yourself
- Regulate your own feelings

Connect

- Through PACE • Comfort
- Help your child calm (co-regulate) • Focus on feelings • Listen • Validate

Correct

- Set limits • Natural consequences (when your child is ready to think about these)
- Talk about what's wrong with the behaviour
- Talk about what other ways your child could have managed the situation
- Suggest alternatives to the behaviour • Help your child learn other ways to express emotions

Repair

- Acknowledge (to yourself and with your child) how difficult that was.
- Say you still love them and will help make things easier.
- Apologise for your role in what happened (e.g. you hadn't noticed how tired they were/hadn't understood what was going on).
- Take responsibility for what you could have done differently.

Reflect

- Reflect on your own and with your child.
- Think about what you could have done differently
- Consider why your child was behaving that way.
- Think about what you will do next time.
- Ask yourself why you found it so hard to manage (if you c
- Ask your child if you missed something.
- Help your child reflect on what happened and link their feelings and behaviours.
- Think about what triggered the behaviour.

I agree with Janet Lansbury about the importance of being able to tolerate your child's big feelings during a tantrum and not just dismiss them, or ignore them.[16] We need to take the feelings driving the behaviour seriously. I do, however, believe that distraction during a meltdown can be helpful if managed well to help diffuse the situation and regain composure. If you do use distraction it is important that this does not make your child think that you don't understand their feelings or accept how difficult they find it to manage them.

When very young, children need adult help to regain control of their emotional and behavioural world. They find it hard to self-soothe and need help to regulate their feelings - it is difficult for them just to ride the storm on their own. Supporting children in the moment is known as *co-regulation* and involves staying with them, empathising (non-verbally as well as verbally), mirroring what they are feeling, and accepting their emotional expression.

When you co-regulate a child's feelings, you can work together at bringing the emotional temperature down. This is a reason that 'time out' is now not generally thought to be a helpful way to manage tantrums in early childhood – children need you when they are distressed. Co-regulation helps the behaviour subside more quickly and shows the child that you are invested in helping them.

Although we often feel the need to impose a sanction after an undesirable behaviour has occurred, we do need to think about who this sanction is for (us or our child?) and how helpful it is. I talked earlier (in the "PACE" section) about natural consequences and would recommend this as the first approach to helping children learn from their behaviour. This certainly reduces the power struggles that so often emerge when other approaches to discipline are adopted. For further ideas on managing tricky behaviour please see "Top Tips" at the end of this handbook.

Managing Yourselves During Tantrums

"If you can control your behaviour when everything around you is out of control, you can model for your children a valuable lesson in patience and understanding...and snatch an opportunity to shape character."
(Jane Clayson Johnson - Author)

It is important to remember, particularly when you are in the midst of chaos, that your child is not having a tantrum to actively try to annoy you. As already highlighted, children do not learn that others have feelings until the age of three or four and the development of this skill depends upon their experience of other people making sense of their emotional world.

For a young child the world is full of novelty; what quickly becomes tedious for us may be extremely exciting for them. Try to see dawdling as exploring and think of how much fun your child is having (even if it's quite boring for you and frustrating when you have lots of things to do).

When your little one is showing tricky behaviour it is up to you to stay calm and to think of rational ways to manage your child's feelings. This is sometimes easier said than done. There have certainly been times that my children's behaviour has made me feel unskilled, helpless, overwhelmed and/or angry; showing this in my own response has normally only made things worse.

You may feel like shouting back, and this may work in the short term. However, if this becomes a pattern of response, this is normally unhelpful in the longer term; children either start to shout back or withdraw and suppress their feelings and behaviour because they are scared or unsure of what your response will be. Whilst the latter may mean your child's behaviour is easier to manage, both reactions can end up creating increasingly stressful and negative cycles. They may also start to learn that their emotional world is unimportant, and that behaviour is all that matters.

If you do get angry with your child then you can always make this better later on (as described earlier, this is called repairing a rupture in your relationship). You can do this by apologising for getting angry, explaining why you felt angry and then giving your child a cuddle (if they'll let you!). In *Stop That Now – I Don't Know How* you see Bartley's dad, who is generally great at taking the PACE approach, becoming frustrated with Bartley. He actively repairs their relationship following this.

Try not to berate yourself if you show your anger occasionally (within reason), but if this becomes a normal response it may be helpful to think about what you may need to do to make some changes. Remember, the way we manage our emotions has a huge impact upon the way our children learn to manage theirs.

The Importance of Play *(as well as Playfulness)*

> *"One of the biggest complaints from adults about their own childhood is the lack of play with their parents."*
> (Margot Sutherland - Child Psychotherapist)

Play is not only an enjoyable part of childhood, but an important one. Through play children develop physically, emotionally, cognitively and creatively. It allows them to engage in the world in a way that feels safe, explore different roles, address their fears, and develop confidence. Children who have time to play, and have parents who actively engage in playing with them, learn about sharing, problem solving and decision-making more quickly then those who don't. Playing with your child also helps you understand their world and lets them know that you are interested in them, both important aspects of developing a secure attachment relationship.

It's important to create a good environment for children to play. Try not to overload your child, but provide toys and varied activities (which stimulate different senses) without too many distractions. Children need to engage in both calming as well as stimulating activities, allowing them to get a sense of the differences between the two and helping them to learn to regulate their feelings.

Do try to follow your child's lead and show enjoyment in playing with them (you need to minimise your own distractions, such as emails, phone calls and working through your ever growing to-do list). Try not to interrupt if they seem to be enjoying something, even if it feels very dull to you - it is normal for a child to play the same game repeatedly, this is an important part of learning.

Play is about exploration, so do not criticise what your child is doing (but do set boundaries if it is unsafe or aggressive). Whilst you should steer away from commands or telling them how to play 'better', you can mirror what they are doing and build upon it for them (known as *scaffolding*), so that they can expand their repertoire of play. Do try to stick to their agenda, not yours, although if your inner child starts coming out, don't worry – I often have to check myself when playing Duplo with my toddler, particularly when he breaks a house that I have spent ages building!

We can all struggle to put play towards the top of the agenda, which I completely understand with the many competing and pressing grown-up tasks we have surrounding us. It may be worth remembering that not only is playing with your child a proven way to promote their development and your relationship with them, but it also gives you a much needed break from your busy schedule, as long as you are able to be in the moment whilst doing it (think of it as a bit of mindfulness practice!).

I am very jealous of my toddler's nanny who has a whole day with him a week - a day without a particular purpose or jobs to do - just a day together. She describes this as therapy for herself – a step away from her normal, busy, life. She is able to be in the moment with him and they can just enjoy each other, slowly playing and exploring the world (whilst I am at work, hmmph!). Not only is this clearly good for her emotional wellbeing, but I can see how much he thrives from his "Lisa days" (to the extent that he waits by the door for thirty minutes before she arrives!).

If you are not particularly comfortable with playing, take it slowly. We all have an imagination in there; it can just take a while to warm up when you are not used to using it regularly, or if you didn't have a very playful childhood yourself. You may be surprised how much fun you can have playing when you allow yourself the time and space for this.

Separation Anxiety

"As a child, I was very careful not to erase my mother's writing on the chalkboard because I would miss her." (Joyce Rachelle - Author)

Whilst a horrible thing to witness, separation anxiety is part of normal development and is common in children between the ages of six months and three years. Separation anxiety develops after a baby understands *object permanence*[17] – the understanding that things exist even when they can't be seen or heard. When your baby learns that they can affect the world with their actions it means they are developing their memory and are not just living in the "now" without awareness of the past and future.

Remembering that you were somewhere a minute ago and then no longer there is clearly going to be very unsettling, particularly when your child has not learnt that you will come back (they can't yet think that far ahead!). Separation anxiety is normally a sign that your child has started to know that they are dependent on the people who care for them, and that they feel safer with you by their side.

One of the key tasks of toddlerhood is to develop independence, whilst, at the same time, being able to return to your *safe base* (secure attachment figure) when things become a bit too much. Not surprisingly therefore, going to a new place without a trusted parent can be very difficult. As you know, toddlers have not always got a calm way of expressing how hard they find things – hence the loud and tearful protests at leaving you. What is key is that we don't join in with these protests. Emotions are contagious (they really are – and physiologically - have a read about *mirror neurons* if you are interested in how this works), so try not to be drawn into your little one's anxiety. Clear explanations and returning when you say you are going to are important actions which you can take to mitigate their anxiety.

Although children generally grow out of it, separation anxiety can last for longer, particularly in children who have experienced loss and a change of caregivers (as I frequently see when working with children who are adopted – see the section on "Children with Additional Needs" at the end of this handbook for more information). In children without additional needs it is rare that separation anxiety continues on a daily basis after the pre-school years, although transitions, tiredness and illness are all likely to increase the feeling at times.

Please Stay Here – I Want You Near provides a way of talking to children about separation from you, and helps them know that it is OK to feel worried by this and that this anxiety is manageable (and you will help them cope with it). It is important that you help your child learn that, although you will leave them, you will come back.

If leaving your child makes you feel very anxious try not to let them see this (easier said than done when you are crying at the door at drop off!) and to remember that you are helping them to learn to cope without you, something that is important for their growing independence. I always take comfort in the fact that my children show this anxiety because they would prefer to be with me, but that, as long as I trust who is looking after them, they will be happy when I have gone. If you really struggle then it may be worth seeing if someone else can drop them at their childcare setting, until they are more settled there and you can feel less anxious about the process. Please see the "Top Tips" at the end of this handbook for further ideas on supporting your child through separation anxiety.

The Arrival of a New Sibling

"Having one child makes you a parent: having two you are a referee."
(David Frost – Journalist and Presenter)

Parents often tell me that they are worried about the impact that having a new baby in the family may have upon their child and how it may affect their relationship. One of the stories in Bartley's Books, *Hey Little Mister - Meet Your Sister!* , deals with supporting your little one through the arrival of a new sibling, and all the changes that this involves.

The arrival of a new sibling often causes feelings of guilt and sadness over changes in our relationship with our first child, as well as worry that we will struggle to cope with their behaviour once the baby has joined the family. Complicating matters is the time the transition to siblinghood occurs - often between the ages of two and three.[18] This is an important period for young children's development. Their emotional and behavioural regulation alongside the emergence of an understanding of others' minds, and the mastery of new skills, makes this a time of change even without the added complication of a new brother or sister.

The additional stress of a newborn sibling may make things harder for the first child, although working out what is normal for the 'terrible twos' and what relates to the baby and changes this involves can be hard to disentangle. Children also respond very differently – there can be a period of disruption and regression, no noticeable changes, or even developmental advances.

Not surprisingly, given how exhausting it is to look after two young children and how our firstborn will experience significant changes (often at a time they thrive on consistency and predictability), older siblings tend to show less affection and can be less responsive to their mothers at the time of transition. There can be changes in mother-child interactions and children have been found to express more negative feelings when with their mothers as compared to before their sibling was born (the research on this is mainly focused on mothers rather than fathers). Furthermore, some evidence has been found for a decrease in maternal warmth and affection, as well as an increase in punitive discipline towards older siblings following the birth of another child.

Don't let this put you off though – it's not all bad news! Research suggests that both mothers and fathers had expected their children's behaviour to be much worse than it actually was once the baby was born. Yes, some were very jealous and showed distress, but others embraced the newcomer, helping out and showing affection towards their little brother or sister. Often it's a bit of both. (See Volling, 2012, for a comprehensive review of research relating to changes in the firstborn following the birth of a sibling.)[19]

Whilst, of course, it will be a big upheaval, when handled sensitively (see "Top Tips" at the end of this handbook for ideas on how to do this), you can continue to have a secure and rewarding relationship with your older child, even if it feels like a backwards step at first. As long as you help your child to make sense of why you need to spend time with the baby, whilst reminding them how they remain very special to you, you can continue to enjoy each other just as much as before.

I remember feeling heart broken and torn between my children when my eldest was two and his little brother had just arrived. I vividly recall him sitting on the stairs saying, "No two boys!" (intimating that I should take his brother back to the hospital immediately!). Luckily, we are still just as close as ever, although I must admit I initially missed spending as much time together with just the two of us. Both children now gain so much from having a brother (even if neither of them will admit it!).

It may never feel like the right time to introduce another child into your family. If you do want another child, it may feel like it is too early, too late, or, sadly, it may never happen. If you do have a new baby and worry about how this is impacting on your firstborn, try to remember the time you spent with them before their sister or brother arrived. The feelings that they hold around this will still be with them, even if they are not showing you this during the early days of the new arrival. If you are a two-parent family, this can also be seen as a time of opportunity for your firstborn to spend more time with their other parent, and to develop their relationship further.

Mastering New Skills and Establishing Routines

Mastering New Skills and Establishing Routines

The majority of this handbook talks about the need to connect with your child and help them make sense of their feelings. This is also true for supporting them to learn new routines and mastering new skills. Bartley's Books include stories focusing upon bedtime routines *(Time For Bed – Rest Your Head)*, healthy eating *(Please Eat Up – No It's Yuck!)*, and toilet training *(You'll Be Happy – Without Your Nappy)*, all providing ways of talking to your children about these areas. One of the most helpful ways to support your child to learn new skills and establish routines is to be clear about your expectations, be consistent in your approach, and to try to stay calm!

It is worth remembering that all children learn new skills at different times, and that all parents teach in their own way. We have different expectations and ideas about how we would like our family to function, and that's OK. It is, however, important to be able to reflect upon what is, and isn't working and whether you are too focused upon achieving a goal before your little one is ready for this.

Try not to compare your child with others. Some sleep through the night early, whilst others struggle to do this. Some will be toilet trained before the age of two, whilst others don't quite get there until four (or older). Some will eat anything you put in front of them, whilst others will refuse any food that is green, or not full of sugar.

If you can focus upon involving your child in developing routines and learning new skills, teaching the importance of them and being consistent in your approach and expectations, you stand a much better chance of getting to where you want to be (or at least somewhere near!).

Bedtime Routines

"Anyone who thinks the art of conversation is dead ought to tell a child to go to bed." (Robert Gallagher - Author)

The story I struggled with the most was the story about bedtime routines. This was because I felt a bit like a fraud. I am a laughing stock amongst my friends…being a child psychologist who advises on issues such as sleep, whilst having children who struggle to fall asleep on their own and to then sleep through the night. All I can really say is I fully empathise with parents struggling in this area and have learnt a lot about what not to do!

If you have read Matthew Walker's book *Why We Sleep*[20] you will be well aware of the importance of sleep (perhaps avoid this one if you have a newborn who is stealing your precious shut eye!). "Sleep hygiene" which involves helping children unwind before they go to bed, promotes sleep and therefore growth and development.[21] There are a number of different components of good sleep hygiene, which I have summarised below:

• Repetitive routines, starting around thiry to forty minutes before sleep.

• Predictable and consistent bedtimes, throughout the week and weekend, if possible.

• Follow recommended sleep times:

 o Twelve to fourteen hours – including naps – for one to three-year-olds

 o Ten to thirteen hours – including naps – for three to five-year-olds

• Avoid electronic devices and television.

• Read or engage in other quiet activities before bed.

• Include positive parent-child interactions.

• A massage and calm music.

• A quiet bedroom.

• Avoid drinks and snacks just before bed (but it's fine to include healthy snacks and a drink at the start of the bedtime routine).

• Provide opportunities for your child to go to sleep and back to sleep on their own.

Obviously you can't always fit all of this in and Mindell and Williamson suggest including two to four activities each night if possible.[22]

Research suggests that children's sleep quality can be positively affected by routine. For example, in infants and toddlers with sleep problems, a three step routine before bed (including a bath, massage and quiet activities, with lights out thirty minutes after the end of bathtime) has been found to result in less waking, shorter periods of waking and decreased time to fall asleep.[23]

Bedtime routines don't just improve sleep quality: their importance goes deeper. The routine, in and of itself, characterises nurturing care and stimulation. Mindell and Williamson's recent review describes how the range of activities involved in bedtime routines, including nutrition (pre-bed snack), hygiene (bath and tooth brushing), communication (talking about your day, reading together) and physical contact (bedtime cuddles) can have a broad ranging impact on both you and your child.

This includes better language, literacy, emotional and behavioural regulation, attachment and family functioning. Three to five-year-olds with good bedtime routines even show better performance in working memory, attention and cognitive flexibility than those without.[24] Bedtime routines are also associated with earlier bedtimes, longer sleep, less awakenings during the night and therefore – for us – better quality sleep, having a positive impact upon our own emotional wellbeing. Hooray!

So, we know the importance of routines before your child gets into bed, but what about them actually getting to sleep? This is often the tricky bit, and can be accompanied by lots of strong feelings (for all of us). Hopefully, with a better bedtime routine the act itself will become easier.

I would love to have a one size fits all, clear message for parents about what to do when you want your child to fall asleep. But I don't. There is hugely differing advice out there, some of which is controversial and believed by many parents to be unhealthy for their child.

We often have lots of questions, with few clear answers, about the best way to support our children to sleep. Do you leave them to cry on their own? Do you sit with them? Do you withdraw slowly? Do you sleep with them? I can see why so many different approaches exist, and how some parents are confused about which way to turn.

I personally have always helped my children get to sleep and co-slept with them when they were little (even my eldest still sometimes hops into bed with me!). I'm aware that this has probably led to me getting less sleep (and therefore sometimes being a less attuned parent), and that their sleep may have suffered too (particularly for my firstborn who I had to check regularly to reassure myself that he was OK, often resulting in me waking him!). However, I know that it fits my parenting approach. They are your children, and it is up to you how you help them learn to sleep.

Whilst I am not going to advocate a specific method of "sleep training", I do like Margot Sutherland's chapter on sleep and bedtimes in her second edition of *What Every Parent Needs to Know* and always try to remember her comment that a parent's "primary goal at bedtime is to bring your child down from a super alert state."[25]

If you are pulling your hair out, rest assured that sleep "problems" are very common. Some studies estimate that around a quarter of children under five have difficulty sleeping, making me wonder whether expectations of "non-problematic" sleep may be slightly misplaced. Whilst this may not help you in moments of exhaustion, at least you will know there are other very tired parents out there too!

Healthy Eating

Even before birth we acquire new likes and dislikes, based upon our mother's diet, so, at birth, children already have preferences for certain tastes. Even the type of milk we offer in infancy can make a difference to children's eating – through breast milk they are exposed to a number of different flavours (which come through the mother's milk), whereas formula fed babies experience less variety. We also have a predisposition not to like bitter tastes (an evolutionary adaptation to protect us against ingesting poison), and, as a result, it can feel like an uphill struggle to get children to eat a variety of healthy foods, particularly vegetables.

The good news is that food preferences can be shaped very quickly through learning, and early childhood is an important time for developing eating habits. In fact, dietary behaviours acquired during the early years of life can extend into adulthood.[26] Whilst food fussiness peaks around the ages of two to five, with children becoming increasingly independent and rejecting of new foods, it is also a time when children are open to developing new preferences.

Children need to try the same food a number of times if they are going to learn to like it: some say three times, others ten, and others twenty - in reality it is likely to relate to your child's previous experiences, your response and their own idiosyncrasies.[27] Interestingly, most parents don't offer a new food more than five times, the message being not to remove it too soon from a child's diet if they don't yet feel able to try it (I'm still working on olives!).

To speed the development of healthy eating along you can try a number of things. Firstly, start early – if your child acquires new tastes before the 'terrible twos' kick in, it can make things easier. It can also be helpful to present food in a variety of forms as we learn through different senses. Let your child see, touch and smell food. Read stories about it - it has been found that picture books are particularly effective when they are interactive[28], so grab a copy of *Please Eat Up – No It's Yuck!* It is also important to praise children for trying new foods, although don't make too much of a fuss about this - we want children to learn that eating vegetables is normal!

The more familiar children are with different foods (and as long as they have a positive association with these), the more likely they are to try them. The British Nutrition Foundation and the University of Reading have developed a short booklet – *See and Eat*.[29] This reminds us how important it is to think about food away from the dinner table, and to include children in learning about vegetables, taking part in growing them, shopping for them and cooking them together.

We know that children will reach for sweet foods whenever they can – try to offer only healthy snacks, and, if you give a choice of snacks, make sure they are both healthy – after all, children will choose the option which is more appealing, familiar and seems safer (to them).[30] It is helpful to remove temptations from the house. If children know that snacks are there and you are restricting them they can become more desirable. Sweets should be offered in moderation and not provided as a reward (I regularly fall into this trap).[31]

So, there are a number of things you can do to support your little one to eat more healthily, but the key to their learning is through your relationship (rather a theme in this handbook!) and your own attitude to food.[32] It has been found that in early childhood, parents provide an important role model in encouraging their children to develop healthy eating and positive body image.[33] Children are like sponges and they will mimic your eating choices, patterns and behaviour related to food. If they see you eating healthily they are more likely to learn to do the same (especially if you show that you enjoy it).[35]

It is, therefore, with your help that your little one will develop a positive relationship with food and learn to eat healthily. As soon as we start pressurising children to eat their food, they will start to feel negative towards it. When a child feels over-controlled their natural internal cues for hunger and fullness are harder for them to notice and respond to. Conversely, children who do not feel pressured instinctively balance their diets.[34] Although young children are pretty good at eating the right amount (if they are feeling non-stressed), do help your child to learn when they are full, name hunger and fullness for them, and try not to put too big a portion on their plate.

Try to take a positive and relaxed approach and bear in mind that it is innate for children to reject vegetables and normal for them to take some time to change this. As some food refusal is natural we need to help children form a new idea of what is safe – how we react determines this. Don't forget that non-verbal communication (such as your facial expressions), is as important as what you say, if not more.

If you're feeling wobbled by your child's difficulties eating healthily try to step back into the PACE approach. When I feel myself becoming frustrated I try to think about how I would feel if I was strapped into a chair and being told to eat something that made me feel anxious and didn't taste nice! It can be easy to get into power struggles over food, but these don't generally result in the outcome you had hoped for.

Some very early research has shown that a child (albeit an older child) is more likely to change their food preferences when observing a fictional hero or friend eating, but not an unknown adult.[36] I have certainly observed my children eating meals they would normally protest about when having friends over and Popeye has massively increased the spinach consumption in our house! Think about how you can use others (fictional or real) to help your child eat more healthily.

As with bedtime routines being beneficial to more than just sleep, family meals contribute to more than just eating healthily. Eating together has been associated with a range of positive outcomes, including higher achievement at school, better self-esteem and resilience.[37] Family mealtimes, therefore, provide opportunities for nutrition and learning about healthy eating, but also enhance social and emotional development.[38]

If you are interested in reading more about healthy eating in early childhood, I highly recommend *The Child Feeding Guide*.[36] This has been developed by academic psychologists and not only provides ideas to encourage children to eat more healthily, but also outlines common pitfalls (and ways to avoid them).

If you are feeling very stuck or worried about your child's health in relation to their diet then it may be worth seeing a dietician, nutritionist or your GP about this.

Toilet Training

Apart from a poo on my (ever forgiving) neighbour's new white carpet, we have been relatively unscathed by the process of toilet training. I have now learnt (by child number three) that the time will come when we are both ready, and that, with a bit of consistency, it can be relatively easy. My third child, now two years and nine months, has been ready for a while, and (probably due to his mother's slowness in taking this forward) has now started to train himself!

In the literature there are two main approaches to potty training – some more regimented and parent led and others more child-led.[39, 40] You can find a helpful summary of these on www.parentingscience.com/potty-training-techniques.html or in Kidoo's paper which outlines different approaches, and advises on when to start toilet training.[41] As far as I am aware, there is no conclusive evidence that one training method is better than another. All approaches suggest starting when the child shows signs of readiness, with some recommending to start at around eighteen months, but only if they seem interested in the process.[42] Others say wait until your child is two or three.

It has been found that encouraging children to try again when not successful is more helpful than focusing primarily on rewards and sanctions. In my work I have seen children being chastised for having 'accidents' – not surprisingly these children seem to struggle the most to master toilet training, associating it with fear and pressure and therefore being less able to learn.

As with helping children learn other skills, a positive and consistent approach is important. Children will learn to be free of nappies at different ages and some will take longer than others to master using a potty/toilet. It is important, as parents, to keep the process light-hearted, despite set backs, and help your child feel as though they are accomplishing something, rather than passing on your frustration if they aren't quite getting it right.

I have included a number of "Top Tips" at the end of the handbook to help you with toilet training. If you are interested in more support then www.uptodate.com/contents/toilet-training-beyond-the-basics provides detailed and frequently updated advice.

Children with Additional Needs

What I love about the PACE approach is how applicable it is to each and every one of us, children and adults alike, regardless of our experiences and needs. Indeed, PACE was initially developed in relation to children who have experienced attachment disruptions and early trauma, and is now being used more broadly - for children with mental health problems and, as here, to inform a general approach to parenting.

Within this handbook I have outlined how important it is to support children to develop an understanding of their feelings and learn how feelings may be influencing their behaviour. Also key is the need for a consistent, positive and light-hearted approach to support young children to develop new skills. All of this is made much easier if we can provide them with a parent who is nurturing and available, who offers connection before correction, and allows time for joint reflection. Again, this is all relevant to children with additional needs.

Children who have experienced trauma and abuse and a change of caregiver struggle more to trust that there are adults who are able to look after them. They are likely to find separations and transitions much more difficult, and find it harder to express what they need. If you're interested in learning more about this, Kim Golding writes about hidden and expressed needs in children who have experienced early trauma.[43]

If you are an adopter or foster carer it can be particularly helpful to focus on your child's developmental rather than chronological age. Ask yourself whether your expectations of them (in terms of acquiring new skills, learning to manage their behaviour, learning to express their feelings and learning to feel safe in relationships) are matched to where they are developmentally. It is always important to think about how much shame they hold from their early experiences (often described as "toxic shame") and how to take the least shaming approach to support recovery and learning. One of your main aims should be to help them understand that struggling to manage their feelings or behaviour does not mean that they are unlovable.

Such children's need for reparative care can take its toll, making it even more important for you to look after yourselves. There is now much more support available for adopters out there – at the time of writing, in the U.K. the Adoption Support Fund is available to every adopted child, making it easier to access specialist therapeutic support for your family.

I feel a bit like I am teaching my grandmother to suck eggs writing this – adoptive parents have taught me so much, and the way I have seen some parents 'story' their child's experiences for them has been just beautiful. When reading Bartley's Books to your child it might be helpful to add to the prompter questions, showing curiosity and acceptance around why they may find certain experiences particularly difficult to manage. For example, in *Please Stay Here – I Want You Near,* Nudge wonders whether Bartley often worries about whether his mother would return, reminding him that she always did. This sort of question could be added to, for example, saying, "In the past your birth mum did not always come back, it must be so hard to believe that I will."

It may also be helpful to share these books with children with additional needs if they are older. I work with an eleven-year-old who spotted *Please Stay Here – I Want You Near* on my desk and insisted that her mum read it to her during one of our sessions. Although the language and lift-the-flaps are aimed at a younger age group she loved it! Clearly, it provided a useful platform to talk about her feelings in a safe and connected way, and to engage in some of those early experiences of reading picture books which she missed as a young child.

Children with learning disabilities may also find it harder to understand and express their feelings and to learn new skills. Their parents are likely to need to provide even more repetition, creativity and ensure good self-care than parents of children without learning disabilities. Again, Bartley's Books may be helpful for older children in this instance, with a focus upon developmental rather than chronological age.

Top Tips

Top Tips

For Separation Anxiety

Top Tips for Separation Anxiety

- If your child is new to being away from you start with **short separations.**

- **Talk to your child about what will happen** at their childcare setting and let them know you will be back at the end (try to make sure you are on time to pick them up).

- Try to ensure you have a **regular routine** before and after childcare. Be predictable in how you drop your child off and leave them.

- **Explain that you are not going away because you don't want to be with your child** but that you have things to do that they can't do with you.

- **Try not to show the anxiety you may feel.** Your child needs to see you as confident as possible to help them feel less anxious.

- If your child is new to being away from you, or separation anxiety has increased, make sure they have **more special time** with you outside of their childcare setting.

- Try to **transfer your child to a member of staff when you leave**, so they have someone they trust to help them manage their feelings of anxiety and so they can see you working together. Make sure you show them that you trust their carer to look after them.

- **Try not to sneak out**, or pretend that you are only leaving briefly (however tempting it may be). It's fine to distract your child with something fun when you leave, as long as you are honest about when you will be back. Try not to make the the goodbye too prolonged.

- It may be helpful for your child to take *a favourite object or toy* which reminds them of you and/or home that helps them to feel more at ease. Taking this with them can reduce the anxiety of separation: psychoanalyst, Donald Winnicott calls this a "transitional object".[46]

- *Take your child's feelings seriously.* Tell them that it is normal to feel worried (and sometimes angry) and talk about the things they will do at their childcare setting which they enjoy.

- *Remember that some children adjust to change more quickly than others*. Don't worry if your child continues to show some anxiety – just go on showing them acceptance of their feelings and be clear about what childcare entails.

- *It will be harder for your child to be without you at some times than others* (such as when tired or unwell, or during changes at home or the childcare setting). This can be really frustrating for parents who think they have conquered it! Try to help your child understand why things are more difficult and explain that they will become easier again.

- *Play "object permanence" games,* such as peek-a-boo and hide-and-seek. This helps your child to learn that things can come and go.

Top Tips

For Tricky Behaviour

Roar

Top Tips for Tricky Behaviour

- *Choose your battles.* Try to ignore minor misdemeanours. Does it really matter if your child doesn't always eat everything or wants to choose their own clothes (however unstylish they look)? Before getting into a power struggle think about what you really feel strongly about and what you can let go. Young children need to have some sense of control over their environment as well as clear boundaries.

- *Try to work out what is behind those tantrums.* Tricky behaviour always communicates something (and the possibilities of what it might be seem endless!), such as hunger, tiredness, boredom, physical illness, worry about change, sadness, needing to know you are available to them, frustration, disappointment, lack of structure, developmental milestones, fear, anger, stress and difficulties at home. Your job is to work out what the particular triggers are this time (it may be more than one) and try to address them. I equate it to trying to work out what a baby is crying for when they're very little – which can take two nappy changes, three attempted naps, some milk and winding to understand!

- *Label what is happening.* If you can guess what is driving your child's behaviour then do – it can be helpful for children to have their behaviours and emotions labelled so that they can make sense of them. Try to explain how their feelings are influencing their behaviour. If you help them understand why they are feeling as they are, for example, because mummy didn't have time to dress all of their dolls exactly as they wanted just before bed, then they will learn to analyse situations and work through them.

  You are still setting a boundary by carrying on with the bedtime routine, but are also helping your child feel understood and more able to make sense of why they got into a rage. This will help your child learn to calm down and problem solve. You will both feel calmer after that and can re-connect. It's fine to return to the labelling later if you need to focus only on calming the situation down at the time.

- Reduce the likelihood of tricky behaviour by *involving your child in decisions*, giving them limited choices where possible.

- **Be consistent and set clear and calm limits.** Set your boundaries, stick to them and explain why you have done so (it is OK to be flexible sometimes; just explain why they have been changed). Have a clear set of family rules so your child knows what to expect. You can make this pictorial to help them understand. Try to ensure you carry out what you say you are going to do (so only say what is realistic!).

- **Try to "externalise" behaviours** and reduce feelings of shame. Talk about your child's behaviour as being tricky or difficult rather than them as being naughty or bad. This can help you address tricky behaviour together, and makes it less likely that they will think about themselves negatively. If you focus too much on the negatives a family narrative can develop that your child is the problem (and if you think you are a problem you tend to behave like one!).

- **Try to be matter-of-fact with difficult behaviour** and not to make your child feel humiliated when they have a meltdown.

- **Create a "yes" environment**. Make your house child friendly and stimulating so that your child can explore without hearing "no" all the time. Obviously we can't always say "yes" – saying "no" is necessary with little children, but do try to do so in moderation. It can feel frustrating and unhelpful for children to be told to stop when they are just being curious and exploring their world (even though it may be getting in the way of our own plans!).

- **Reward desirable behaviour and try not to punish the negative** (let children learn through natural consequences instead). Children learn more quickly this way and life feels more relaxed and enjoyable. If you are using rewards to encourage desirable behaviour it is important to offer the right ones. A younger child cannot wait for a reward and will need an instant positive experience (this does not have to be an object – it could be extra time with you or simply a hug or high five).

For example, when they help to put the toys away you can praise them and let them know that you have extra time for some fun because they were so helpful. An older child may tolerate waiting for a reward, and some parents find sticker charts helpful but it's important that the goal is achievable and the implementation consistent. I would always try to focus upon connecting and correcting rather than placing a sticker on a chart that does not directly relate to the behaviour in question.

- **Try not to use 'time out'** (unless *you* really need this!). Helping your child work out what went wrong and learn how not to repeat the behaviour is generally more constructive. I sometimes use 'time out' as a last resort, primarily when I am struggling to control my annoyance at my children's behaviour (making this more of a tool to manage me than them).

- **If you do get angry with your child then you can always make this better later.** You do this by apologising for getting angry, explaining why, and then giving your child a cuddle.

- Show your child that it is **good to express their feelings and desires** and teach them alternative (less disruptive) ways of doing so.

- **Try not to catch your child's emotional chaos** (remember it's a tricky phase, breathe deeply and have a good self-care plan), think about the following steps:
  o Step back and **notice your feelings**.
  o **Connect** with your child.
  o **Redirect /correct** their behaviour.
  o **Repair** your relationship after moments of disconnection.
  o **Reflect** with them about what happened (in a light-hearted way at the right time).

This may sound like a lot to remember in the moment, but it is much easier to put into place if you do step back and think about what you are going to do before going in guns blazing! Some of my clients have notes on their fridge, some with PACE phrases and others with these steps for managing tricky behaviour in the moment.

Top Tips

For the Arrival of a New Sibling

Top Tips for the Arrival of a New Sibling

- *Prepare your child* for what is going to happen. Be honest – don't just talk about the good things, or start describing the baby as a playmate. That takes a while!

- *Don't rush your child into mastering new skills* before the baby is born.

- *Let your child know that you may be away* for a while when you have the baby and who will be looking after them. See if you can keep as normal a routine as possible.

- When the baby is born it can help to *encourage positive feelings* if they give your older child a present (my eldest still treasures the toy car his baby brother gave to him in hospital).

- *Remind your older child that there will be lots of changes* and that they may not like some of them. They may expect things to go back to normal after the baby is born.

- Ask visitors to *fuss over both children* so that your older child experiences positive feelings (and hopefully relates this to your new arrival).

- *Promote discussion about new babies across settings* – for example, take photos of the new baby to their childcare setting/school.

- *Spend additional special time with your oldest* after the baby is born (easier said than done, but try to snatch some moments).

- *Talk to your older child about how they may be feeling.* They may feel on the outside of a unit they were part of. If they are negative towards the new arrival help them understand how it is normal to be jealous (but still set expectations around behaviour).

- ***Try not to compare your children.*** Your older child may already feel in direct competition or fear that there is not enough love to go around. This may increase their negative feelings (and therefore behaviour) towards the new baby.

- Expect your older child to be ***more demanding and/or to regress.*** Other common patterns of behaviour include hostility (covert or overt), becoming withdrawn and moodiness. Try not to get annoyed with these; they are natural ways of getting your attention and expressing feelings.

- ***Remember it is normal to be exhausted.*** If you are more irritable (which sleep deprivation contributes to massively) don't be cross with yourself. Just help your older child understand that this is not because of them.

- ***Try to foster a positive sibling relationship*** between your older child and the new baby. You can do this by giving your older child a role in helping with the baby (within reason!), and also by pointing out when the baby notices, reacts to and smiles at them.

- ***Consider your older child's developmental stage.*** Difficulties or changes in your relationship may not all be related to having a new sibling (even if having a new baby feels as though everything is standing still!).

- ***Try not to feel guilty or worried*** about your relationship with your older child when you have to focus so much on your new baby. Remember that you have spent a lot of individual time with them, which they will have internalised through developing a template of your relationship (known as an *internal working model*), seeing you as predictable, reliable and loving.

- Try to remember that ***having a sibling is likely to be an important and fulfilling relationship*** for your older child in the longer term, even though it may not feel like it when the baby arrives (and for quite some time afterwards)!

Top Tips

For Bedtime Routines

Top Tips for Bedtime Routines

- Try to ensure your child gets enough *exercise during the day* - outside if possible.

- *Try not to put your child straight to bed after a big meal* - if they are hungry then give them a light, healthy snack at the beginning of the bedtime routine.

- *Have a regular winding down routine.* Leave time to relax together after having a bath and brushing teeth (which can, in themselves, be a battle). During this time it can be helpful to:

  o Read a book together.

  o Cuddle up together.

  o Make the room darker.

  o Put on some quiet, calming music.

  o Give your child a massage (if my eldest is struggling to sleep a gentle neck massage works a treat every time).

  o Get the room temperature right.

- *Try to keep a sense of humour and to stay calm yourself.* I know this is hard to do when you are shattered. However, when I have become outwardly frustrated at my children because they are not sleeping, I am back to square one and have to start the calming down process (for all of us) all over again.

- *If your child is finding it harder to sleep than normal, try to think what this may relate to.* Have there been recent changes? Are they struggling with something during the day? Try to talk with your child about this: guess what may be going on for them and see if any of these reasons ring true.

- Help your child learn to **recognise the signs of tiredness and the benefits of sleep.** If they have slept well make a big song and dance about it and comment upon how much happier they are the next day.

- If your child sleeps in their own room/bed and wakes regularly during the night, you may want to **leave something that smells of you in their bed** (a "transitional object") and let them know that it is safe to go back to sleep without you and that you are near.

- It can be helpful to **stay in the room when your child is falling asleep**; either lying next to them or making yourself busy tidying up (some disagree with this and suggest you should be away and let your child fall asleep without you in the room).

- If your child is **scared of the dark keep some light on.** If they get regular nightmares then talk about these with them during the day; help them learn that these are only in their imagination and are not going to come true. I put up dream catchers for my children, they have their favourite brave toys in bed, and I talk them through other ways to end the bad dreams - all of which works well.

Top Tips

For Healthy Eating

Top Tips for Healthy Eating

- *Make mealtimes calm.* Remove distractions and try not to show anger if your child won't eat a dish which you have slaved over (I decided not to spend hours cooking in the early days so that I would not get annoyed if my children refused to eat it).

- *Have routines and clear expectations* about behaviour at mealtimes (these are often very different within families).

- *Try to avoid offering your child bribes* and not to focus too much on your child eating their greens (although a bit of praise for trying new foods can be helpful). Without making a big deal of it children are more likely to learn that eating healthy food is what's expected, and less likely to consider vegetables as different from the rest of their food.

- *Remember that excitement, tiredness, illness and so on can affect appetite.* You may need to adjust your expectations at these times, or schedule mealtimes to minimise these impacting on their eating.

- *Choose your battles and remember what works.* I find it very annoying when my two year old will only eat with a matching plate and spoon, and only if the spoon is not "wonky donkey" (I have no idea why!). He eats much more when he has this unusual requirement catered for, so I go with it. Sometimes just little things like this can help a child enjoy their food more.

- *Don't give snacks before a meal or let your child fill up with sugary drinks.* Try to feed your child only when they are hungry and to keep portions small enough – you can always offer more, but big portions may put them off.

- *Let your child be involved in the process* through growing vegetables, shopping with you, helping you cook and serving food (under your direction). Children are more likely to try something which they have been involved with, have some control over, and gain a sense of success from.

- **Try to make mealtimes fun** (without over-excitement) and **be imaginative**: our sweetcorn cobs are pretend skyscrapers with lots of windows (which we try to eat individually) and we often make faces from a variety of foods and eat different parts of them (pretending not to be able to see when the eyes have been eaten!).

- **Try not to frown on mess**, however frustrating it is. It is helpful for children to learn independence by feeding themselves. They can always help you tidy it up though!

- **Don't punish poor eating** or make your child feel guilty if they don't finish their food. When children associate mealtimes with negative feelings they are likely to be less inclined to try new foods and less able to notice signs of fullness and hunger.

- **Remember that children are different**: some are more adventurous at trying new foods, others not so much; work out what your child will eat and work around that. Don't compare your child's eating with others – my eldest was a dream and I thought it was because I had encouraged healthy eating so well, until my second came along! Don't label your child as being a bad eater or not liking the food - we often live up to others' expectations of us.

- **If your child rejects a particular food offer it again another time.** If your child really objects to eating vegetables, try to change the presentation or texture, for example, blending them to make soup (which they can enjoy dipping bread into). Try adding flavours to help your child with unfamiliar or bitter vegetables.

- **Offer a balanced diet and enough choice.** There are lots of ways we can help children get what they need; it can just take a lot of experimentation and determination on our part.

- **Model healthy eating.** Children learn a lot from observing their parents' habits. Try to reflect upon your own relationship with food and try not to pass on unhealthy attitudes.

- **Talk about the benefits of healthy food** and link these to your child's eating. This can be done through books, songs, role play, pictures and so on.

Top Tips

For Toilet Training

Top Tips for Toilet Training

- *Wait until your child is ready.* Signs of this include some (or all) of the following:
  o Following simple instructions.
  o Using words such as "poo" and "wee".
  o Copying others using the toilet.
  o Wanting to be independent.
  o Being able to pull pants up and down.
  o Having dry periods for three to four hours.
  o Showing a dislike of being in a dirty nappy.

- *Try to explain the process:*
  o Through books (such as *You'll Be Happy – Without Your Nappy!*).
  o Show your child where their bowel movements go. Some parents find it helpful to take their child to the toilet and empty the nappy into the toilet bowl.
  o Let them watch you doing it (if you feel comfortable with this).
  o Show them one of the dolls that drinks and does a wee into a toy potty.

- *Create a routine:*
  o Start changing their nappy in the bathroom if you didn't before so they associate this with bowel movements.
  o Sit them on the potty or toilet once or twice a day, when they are likely to have a poo (try to do this after meals).
  o Include them in dressing themselves and washing their hands afterwards.

- *Try to instil some fun.* For example, let your child help to choose a potty that they like or a toilet seat and little step.

- *Help your child notice their bodily feelings* through commenting when they look like they need the toilet and where they may feel this (e.g. in their tummy).

- *Remind your child regularly* that they can go to the potty/toilet, especially when they are fully immersed in an activity (which you may have to help them stop for a try on the potty) or feeling particularly tired. You quickly get a sense of how regularly they need to go and how much prompting they may or may not need.

- *Use praise* (for trying as well as successful attempts). Children learn through positive feedback and will feel more motivated to achieve when they get this.

- *Don't get angry about accidents.* Instead, calmly clean up and suggest that next time they use the potty or toilet instead.

- *Try not to show frustration* (even though it is frustrating when you have a million things to do and your child is sitting on the potty doing nothing – and doesn't until you put their nappy back on!). It is very hard to poo when you are feeling uptight.

- *Remember it can take some time to be fully potty trained and there may be relapses.* Try to schedule in when most convenient for you; many parents like the summer months where children can walk around without a nappy more easily.

- Let your child know that you *can take them to the toilet whenever they think they need it* (be prepared for many visits without 'success'). When you are out show your child where the bathroom is.

- You will know when they are *ready for night training* when they are going through the night with a dry nappy relatively regularly (although parents often approach day and night training at the same time).
  o Don't let them drink too much before bed.
  o Tell them if they wake they can call you to help get a potty, or leave it by the bed for when they want to use it.

Top Tips

For Parents

Top Tips for Parents

- Take a **P**layful, **A**ccepting, **C**urious and **E**mpathic approach to parenting (and to yourself).

- Try to take responsibility for reconnecting with your child after a **rupture** in your realtionship and for **repair.**

- Stay **open and available** to your child, even if they are resisting your care.

- Remember how powerful **non-verbal communication** is and how, particularly during moments of distress, young children focus much more on this than what you are saying.

- Encourage your child to **show their feelings** and try not to dismiss them. Redirect their behaviours but not feelings.

- Try to focus upon moments of **positive connection** with your child. Keep a memory jar of these special moments and look at them when times are tough.

- If there are two of you parenting, try to take a **unified approach.** Whilst this can be difficult, acknowledge your differences and reflect upon what works best for all of you.

- Remember that even though you are **always trying to do your best**, there will be times when your best does not feel good enough.

- However hard it is when surrounded by other parents comparing their child's milestones, **try not to worry what others think about you** and your child.

- Don't underestimate the importance of your **own self-care**, and remember that it is helpful for both you and your child.

- If there are **patterns emerging** that you don't like in the way that you are parenting, or in the way that your child is responding to you, have a think about what this may be about. Is there something outside your relationship that you or your child are struggling with? Is there something that you are inadvertently repeating from your own childhood? What buttons are they pushing for you and where did they came from?

- If you notice that you are struggling much more than normal, feeling very low or anxious, or finding it hard to bond with your little one, **talk to someone you trust**. It may also be helpful to seek professional support.

- **Be kind to yourself.** Try to reduce the "should haves" and the other things you do to convince yourself that you are not getting it right, and are not a good parent. Your child will love you even when you make mistakes.

- **Try some mindfulness.** I know that this can sometimes feel like a bit of a panacea for helping you with any emotional experience, but it really can be useful in stopping your mind going at a million miles an hour, in unhelpful circles, and to help your body feel calmer.

- Remember that we **all need to have connections with others**. Having a little one can feel all consuming, and reduce the amount of time we have to see other adults. We can feel refreshed and remember other parts of ourselves outside of parenting when we have supportive relationships outside the immediate family. Try to fit in at least a bit of a social life if you can.

- Try to **enjoy the good times**. Although it can feel like the tricky times are taking over our lives, it is true what grandparents say about time flying by. They'll be teenagers before you know it!

About the Author

Dr Sarah Mundy, Consultant Clinical Psychologist
BSc (Hons), MSc, DClinPsy

Sarah has been inspired and influenced by a number of people, many of whose ideas are reflected in this book. Psychology's great potential for good, she believes, resides in the variety of positive changes it can bring to families, relationships and wider social groups. She has always had an interest in people and relationships, so her path into applied psychology was an obvious one. After a first degree in Psychology and Zoology she undertook a Masters in Forensic Psychology and was subsequently awarded her Doctorate in Clinical Psychology at University College, London in 2004.

Following her heart, Sarah relocated to Cornwall in 2005 - a county rich in memories from her childhood. Since then, she has specialised in working with children and families, both within statutory public services and the independent sector, culminating as a director of a large psychology practice. As her family grew, Sarah realised she was being pulled in too many directions (and not managing in any of them particularly well!), so followed her ambition to find a better balance between working as a psychologist and enjoying being a mum.

In 2018, therefore, she established her own company, Amicus Psychology, through which she continues to practise as a Consultant Clinical Psychologist. As well as having more time with her three young children, Sarah has been able to focus on her longstanding dream of bringing Parenting Through Stories to life. Writing the children's books has taken her back to her father's imaginative storytelling when she was a child, and the moments of joy and connection this brought.

Now working primarily in adoption, Sarah helps children and their parents to develop more secure attachment relationships. Together, they make sense of difficult early experiences and consider how these may have affected a child's ability to let their new parents look after them and how to move forward as a family. Her therapeutic work is based upon Dyadic Developmental Psychology, which is underpinned by the PACE approach. By embedding the guiding principles of PACE in Bartley's Books and the accompanying *Parenting Handbook* her aim is to support families to put this theory successfully, and enjoyably, into practice. Sarah firmly believes that stories, whether they are about a child's own experiences, or those of others, are key to helping children through difficult times.

About the Illustrator

Rachel Millson-Hill, illustrator
BSc (Hons), PGCE

Rachel has had a passion for art since she could first hold a crayon. She spent most of her childhood painting and drawing on anything that she thought made a suitable canvas (including the walls of her bedroom!)

As a teenager she won various art prizes in school and in her county. However, in a bid to keep herself grounded in the real world, she studied for a business degree at Loughborough University. Outside lectures, she spent every spare second behind an easel with a paint brush in her hand and a pencil tucked behind her ear. Whilst her fellow students adorned themselves with suitcases and even wore suits to lectures, Rachel turned up to Statistics in paint-splattered purple jeans and a holey woollen jumper down to her knees.

After completing her degree, Rachel moved down to Cornwall and began life as a professional artist exhibiting abstract oil paintings of the sea in galleries around the South West. However, as technology progressed, she began to do more digital design and illustration on her trusty Apple Mac and attracted a growing number of corporate clients. Since then, she has worked with a wide variety of businesses from all over the world, designing ranges of clothing, packaging, corporate branding, character designs and now children's books.

Describing the technical details of her work illustrating Bartley's Books, she says: "After sketching and doodling ideas with a pencil and watercolours, I used a surface pro pen to illustrate directly onto the screen. I then used a mixture of Adobe design programmes to add texture and shading, so as to bring the characters and scenes to life".

References

[1] For example, Carey, T. & Rudkin, A. (2019) *What Is My Child Thinking?: Practical Child Psychology for Modern Parents*. DK Publishing.

[2] DanielHughes.org

[3] Agosto, D. E. (2013) Educational and Social/Emotional Benefits of Oral Storytelling. *Storytelling, Self, Society*, 9 (1), 53-76.

[4] Kim, Y. Petermeier, H. (2016) *Family Storytelling and the Benefits for Children Fact Sheet* 16-07, University of Nevada.

[5] Erickson, E. (2018) *Effects of Storytelling on Emotional Development*. Retrieved from Sophia, the St. Catherine University repository website: https://sophia.stkate.edu/maed/256.

[6] Scheff, T., Phillips, B. & Kincaid, H. (2006) Goffman Unbound!: A New Paradigm for Social Science (The Sociological Imagination). Paradigm Publishers.

[7] Siegal, D. & Payne-Bryson, T. (2011) *The Whole-Brain Child. 12 Proven Strategies To Nurture Your Childs Developing Mind*. Penguin Random House Publishing.

[8] Hughes, D. & Baylin, J. (2012) *Brain-Based Parenting: The Neuroscience of Caregiving for Healthy Attachment*. W. W. Norton and Company Publishing.

[9] Bowlby, J. (1969) *Attachment and Loss, Volume 1*. New York: Basic Books Publisher.

[10] Siggins, K. & Taberner, K. (2015) *The Power of Curiosity How to Have Real Conversations That Create Collaboration, Innovation and Understanding*. Morgan James Publishing.

[11] Golding, K. (2017) *Everyday Parenting with Security and Love: Using PACE to Provide Foundations for Attachment*. Jessica Kingsley Publishing.

[12] Astington, J. & Edward, M. (2010) The Development of Theory of Mind in Early Childhood. In: Tremblay RE, Boivin M, Peters RDeV, eds. Zelazo PD, topic ed. *Encyclopedia on Early Childhood Development* [online]. http://www.child-encyclopedia.com/social-cognition/according-experts/development-theory-mind-early-childhood.

[13] Ruffman et al, (1999) How parenting style affects false belief understanding. *Social Development*. 8 (3), 395-411.

[14] Sutherland, M. (2016) *The Science of Parenting: How Todays Brain Research Can Help You Raise Happy, Emotionally Balanced Children*. DK Publishers.

[15] Payne-Bryson, T. & Siegal, D. (2015) *No Drama Discipline; The Best-Selling Parenting Guide To Nurturing Your Childs Developing Mind*. Bantam Publishing.

[16] Lansbury, J. (2014) *No Bad Kids; Toddler Discipline Without Shame*. CreateSpace Independent Publishing.

[17] Piaget, J. (1954). The development of object concept (M. Cook, Trans.). In: J. Piaget & M. Cook (Trans.) *The Construction of Reality in the Child*. Basic Books, pp. 3–96.

[18] Baydar, N., Greek, A. & Brooks-Gunn, J. (1997) A Longitudinal Study of the Effects of the Birth of a Sibling during the First 6 Years of Life. *Journal of Marriage and Family*.

[19] Volling, B. (2012) Family Transitions Following the Birth of a Sibling: An Empirical Review of Changes in the Firstborn's Adjustment. *Psychological Bulletin*. 138 (3), 497–528.

[20] Walker, M. (2017) *Why We Sleep*. Simon and Schuster Publishing.

[21] Hall, W. & Nethery, E (2018) What does Sleep Hygiene have to offer Children's Sleep Problems? *Paediatric Respiratory Reviews*. In: Importance of good sleep routines for children. Science Daily, University of British Columbia.

[22] Mindell, J. & Williamson. A. (2018) Benefits of a Bedtime Routine in Young Children: Sleep, Development, and Beyond. *Sleep Medicine Review*. 40, 93-108.

[23] Mindell, J., Meltzer, L. & Carskadon, M. (2009) Developmental aspects of sleep hygiene: findings from the 2004 National Sleep Foundation Sleep in America Poll. *Sleep Med*. 10 (7), 771-9.

[24] Kitsaras, G., Goodwin, M., Allan, J., Kelly, M. & Pretty, I. (2018) Bedtime routines, child wellbeing & development. *BMC, Public Health*. 18, 386.

[25] Sutherland, M. (2016) *The Science of Parenting: How Todays Brain Research Can Help You Raise Happy, Emotionally Balanced Children*. DK Publishing. p.66.

[26] Nekitsing, C., Blundell-Birtill, P. & Cockrof. J., (2018) Systematic review and meta-analysis of strategies to increase vegetable consumption in preschool children aged 2-5 years. *Appetite*. 127, 138-154.

[27] Wardle et al (2003) Increasing children's acceptance of vegetables: a randomized trial of parent-led exposure. *Appetite*. 40 (2), 155-162.

[28] de Droog, S., Buijzen, M. & Valkenburg, P. (2014) Enhancing Children's Vegetable Consumption using vegetable promoting picture books. The impact of interactive-shared reading and character-product congruence. *Appetite*. 73, 73–80.

[29] British Nutrition Foundation & University of Reading: https://www.nutrition.org.uk/healthyliving/toddlers/eatveg.html see and eat encouraging your preschool child to eat vegetables, a practical guide.

[30] Anzman-Fransca, S., Ventury, A., Ehrenberg, S & Myers, K. (2017) Promoting healthy food preferences from the start: a narrative review of food preference learning from the prenatal period through early childhood. *Obesity Review*. 19(4), 576-604.

[31] Child Feeding Guide (2017). www.childfeedingguide.co.uk. University of Loughborough.

[33] Liu, Y. & Stein, M. (2013) Feeding Behaviour of Infants and Young Children and Its Impact on Child Psychosocial and Emotional Development. Child Nutrition. *Encyclopedia on Early Childhood Development.*

[34] Hart, L., Damiano, S., Cornell, C & Paxton, S. (2015) What parents know and want to learn about healthy eating and body image in preschool children: a triangulated qualitative study with parents and Early Childhood Professionals. *BMC Public Health.* 15, 596.

[35] Fisher, J., Mitchell, D., & Smicklas-Wright. (2002) Parental Influences on young girls' fruit and vegetable, micronutrient and fat intakes. *Journal of the American Dietetic Association.* 102 (12), 58-64.

[36] Child Feeding Guide (2017). www.childfeedingguide.co.uk. University of Loughborough.

[38] Duncker, K. (1938) Experimental Modification Of Children's Food Preferences Through Social Suggestion. *Journal of Abnormal Social Psychology.* 33, 489-507.

[39] https://www.pz.harvard.edu/projects/the-family-dinner-project.

[40] Liu, Y. & Stein, M. (2013) Feeding Behaviour of Infants and Young Children and Its Impact on Child Psychosocial and Emotional Development. Child Nutrition. *Encyclopedia on Early Childhood Development.*

[41] Azrin, N. & Foxx R(1974) *Toilet training in less than a day.* Pocket Books Publishers.

[42] Brazelton, T., & Sparrow, J.D. (2004) *Toilet training the 'Brazelton way'.* Cambridge, MA: De Capo Press.

[43] Kiddoo, D. (2012) Toilet training in children: when to start and how to train. *CMAJ.* 184 (5), 511.

[44] American Academy of Sleep Medicine (2016). A consensus statement of the American Academy of Sleep Medicine. *Journal of Clinical Sleep Med.* 12 (6), 785–786.

[45] Golding, K. (2015) Connection Before Correction: Supporting Parents to Meet the Challenges of Parenting Children who have been Traumatised within their Early Parenting Environments. *Children Australia, Volume 40.*

[46] Winnicott, D. (1953) Transitional Objects and Transitional Phenomena – A Study of the First Not-Me Possession. *International Journal of Psycho-Analytics.* 34, 89-97.

Reviews

"This series is sure to delight young children and parents/caregivers alike. Dr. Sarah Mundy along with illustrator Rachel Millson-Hill provide a delightful and creative platform for parents together with their children to name, explore and organise typical developmental experiences and feelings that children encounter. While this series is written for general parenting it is very applicable to parenting those children who have experienced trauma. The accompanying parenting handbook is easy to read, full of solid resources for parents who are engaged in the most humbling, exhausting, and enriching task – parenting and guiding a child into becoming an adult. The children books are inviting, the images colourful, the characters relatable and along with the parenting guidebook the whole package makes for a fantastic series and invaluable resource. Woven throughout the stories and handbook is Dr. Daniel Hughes' PACE (playful, accepting, curious, and empathetic) attitude. As I like to say, PACE is good for all, but essential for some!"

Betty J.B. Brouwer, Chair of DDPI Board DDP Network

"*Please Stay Here- I Want You Near* is ideal for young children and or those with Special Educational Needs who are starting nursery, preschool or primary school. This beautifully illustrated, lift the flap children's book tells the story of a loveable bear called Bartley, who likes school but is a bit apprehensive about going. Through clever questions hidden behind flaps in the book, children are gently invited to open up about their own feelings about starting school or nursery. What I particularly loved about this book is it's underpinned by psychology and experience. The author, Dr Mundy, is not only a Consultant Clinical Psychologist, but she's also a mum of three children. So not only does she have the professional understanding and experience of how children develop and express their emotions, but she also has the lived experience of raising children herself. The final pages of the book provide parents with top tips on separation anxiety, such as when leaving a child at school/nursery not sneaking out without them realising."

SEN Resources Blog

"There are few good books that reflect the reality of young children's lives. Sarah's books do this and give us something special. They help adults share stories with children when life is scary or uncertain. Sarah provides books to capture the interest of children as well as a helpful book for parents. Sarah's books include how to use PACE, a light, curious, spontaneous way of communicating that engages and connects with children. DDP Connects UK (CIC) is pleased to support Sarah and appreciates her hard work in producing these books."

Julie Hudson, DDP Connects UK

"Stories are so important for children, but it can be really difficult to find children's books that reaffirm the messages, that, as a Child Psychologist, I believe are so important to instill in our children. These messages include:
• That our children are safe
• That adults notice when they are struggling
• That adults will soothe and support them at times of difficulty

These are the messages that we need our children to grow up believing. This is the basis of a secure attachment. Decades of research links secure attachment to a myriad of positive outcomes for children.

What I love about Dr Sarah Mundy's book, and Rachel Millson-Hill's engaging illustrations, is, not only do the characters deliver these messages through their interactions with Bartley Bear, but, with the support of Nudge the squirrel, the child is supported, with their parent, to notice and problem-solve the ways in which adults can help them feel safe and secure.

Dr Mundy has produced an accompanying handbook which succinctly explains a parenting approach that Dan Hughes developed to support secure attachment, the PACE Model. This encourages parents to "try out some ideas" outside of the storytelling process. For me, this is the magic of what Sarah has created. These resources are a valuable tool for parents to understand and apply an evidence-based approach to helping family members feel safe and connected."

Dr Kimberley Bennett, Child, Adolescent and Educational Psychologist

Acknowledgements

I started this project on my own, with an idea I really wanted to put into practice, but without really knowing how to do so. Instead of taking the traditional publishing route, I ended up working with a local group of self-employed mums. That's when it really started to take shape! There is no way this would have found its way into print without them. I have been humbled by how committed they have all been to the project, working around the clock to meet tight deadlines, despite juggling little ones, big ones and day jobs.

Rachel Millson-Hill, illustrator, has never questioned my requests for different versions of logos and characters, nor expressed frustration when I have decided to go back to the original (sorry, Rach!). We only settled on Bartley being a bear after she had created lots of other beautifully designed characters including a chameleon, a little boy and a rabbit. I can't believe how wonderfully Rachel has translated Bartley's Books into pictures, capturing parent-child relationships and emotions so sensitively.

Claire Payne has worked tirelessly and persistently to promote the project, never doubting we would get there. She has helped me stumble my way through the craziness of social media, and has introduced me to new names in the parenting world. Our toddlers have truly bonded over this project, as have we.

Rebecca Ritson has been an editing whizz, grasping the concepts in the books within minutes, and reviewing various versions of my ramblings, always bringing me back down to earth and cutting down on the psychobabble! Her blogs on the Parenting Through Stories website have been just beautiful, enlightening me about the power of words. Her descriptions of personal experience, which must have, at times, felt exposing to write, have really highlighted the importance of connecting with your own experiences if you are to help your children through the muddles of life.

My little sister, Emily, a playful soul, helped me immensely with the stories, at a time they needed an injection of some much needed creativity. My other sister, Helen, wonderfully organised and practical, has been there for me along the way, providing useful suggestions and support. I would also like to thank my old family friend, Adam, for creating the Crowdfunding campaign video. This took me back to the family films we used to make on holiday together, albeit much more professional this time!

Henrie and Jenni, two of my oldest school friends, have helped me so much, noticing what I needed (often before I did!) and generously sharing their time and expertise. A massive thanks to both of you.

Thanks also to Kim Golding and Julie Hudson, two fantastic Clinical Psychologists working to promote PACE across the UK. Given how busy they both are I very much appreciate the time they took to review and comment on Parenting Through Stories. It helped my imposter syndrome no end! And, of course, to Maxine Tostevin, who has been my unconditionally supportive psychology mentor (and good friend) over the last fifteen years.

Finally, the hugest of thanks to Al, my long-suffering partner. Thank you for putting up with me going on, and on, and on, about Parenting Through Stories for almost a decade. (I'm afraid it may carry on for some time!). It wouldn't have got this far without you.

Bartley's Books

Thank you for reading this book - I do hope that you have enjoyed it and that the ideas have been applicable to, and helpful in, everyday life with your little ones. If you are interested in putting some of the theory outlined in this handbook into practice through storytelling, why not read Bartley's Books with your child?

There are six interactive children's stories in the corresponding Bartley's Books series. These help you explore your child's experiences with them, encouraging them to express their feelings, master new skills, feel closer to you, and cope with everyday challenges together.

The books cover the following areas:
- **Separation Anxiety** – *Please Stay Here - I Want You Near*
- **Tricky Behaviour** – *Stop That Now - I Don't Know How*
- **The Arrival of a New Sibling** – *Hey, Little Mister - Meet Your Sister!*
- **Healthy Eating** – *Please Eat Up – No! It's Yuck!*
- **Toilet Training** – *You'll be Happy - Without Your Nappy*
- **Bedtime Routines** – *Time for Bed - Rest Your Head*

To give you a taste of the stories, with Rachel Millson-Hill's captivating illustrations, a sample is included on the final pages of this book. I hope that you and your children enjoy the characters and that, with your help, they will be able to relate the stories to their own experiences.

Dr Sarah Mundy
Consultant Clinical Psychologist
Author and Creator of Parenting Through Stories

This is
Bartley Bear

He isn't very old–
Mostly he is happy,
sometimes he is bold.

When Bartley's in a **muddle,**

he doesn't know what to do.
He needs some help from Mum or Dad—
Does he sound a bit like you?

Hi there! I'm Nudge.

Do you want to
hear a story
about Bartley...?